WONDERS OF CANADA

Old Town Lunenburg

Jennifer Howse

Weigl

CALGARY
www.weigl.com

Published by Weigl Educational Publishers Limited
6325 10th Street SE
Calgary, Alberta
T2H 2Z9

Website: www.weigl.com

We acknowledge the financial support of the Government of Canada through the Book Publishing
Industry Development Program (BPIDP) for our publishing activities.

Library and Archives Canada Cataloguing in Publication

Howse, Jennifer
     Old Town Lunenburg / Jennifer Howse.

(Wonders of Canada)
Includes index.
ISBN 978-1-55388-395-1 (bound)
ISBN 978-1-55388-396-8 (pbk.)

     1. Old Town Lunenburg World Heritage Site (N.S.)--Juvenile literature.
2. Lunenburg (N.S.)--Juvenile literature. 3. World Heritage areas--Nova
Scotia--Lunenburg--Juvenile literature. I. Title. II. Series.
FC2349.L85H69 2007   j971.6'23   C2007-902261-8

Printed in the United States of America
1 2 3 4 5 6 7 8 9 0 11 10 09 08 07

Photograph Credits

Project Coordinator
Leia Tait

Design
Terry Paulhus

Contents

Model Town by the Sea 4

Where in the World? 6

A Trip Back in Time 8

Becoming a World Heritage Site 10

World Heritage in Canada 12

Natural Wonders 14

Cultural Treasures 16

Amazing Attractions 18

Issues in Heritage 20

Plan a Model Town 22

Quiz/Further Research 23

Glossary/Index 24

Model Town by the Sea

Imagine sailing along the east coast of Nova Scotia. Your boat enters a deep harbour where great, wooden ships rest on the water. Brightly painted wood buildings line the shore. They form a hill of red, blue, and green rising away from the shoreline. The scene has changed little since these structures were first built more than 250 years ago.

This is Old Town Lunenburg. It is North America's best example of a planned **colonial** settlement. It is also a hub of Canadian seafaring **culture**. Lunenburg was once a major fishing and shipbuilding centre. Today, it is known for its colourful old buildings. These structures provide a strong link to the town's past. Old Town Lunenburg has an important place in Canadian and world history. It was named a World Heritage Site in 1995.

■ The historic look of Old Town Lunenburg keeps the area's history alive.

What is a World Heritage Site?

Heritage is what people inherit from those who lived before them. It is also what they pass down to future generations. Heritage is made up of many things. Objects, traditions, beliefs, values, places, and people are all part of heritage. Throughout history, these things have been **preserved**. A family's heritage is preserved in the stories, customs, and objects its members pass on to each other. Similarly, a common human heritage is preserved in the beliefs, objects, and places that have special meaning for all people, such as Old Town Lunenburg.

The United Nations Educational, Scientific and Cultural Organization (UNESCO) identifies places around the world that are important to all people. Some are important places in nature. Others are related to culture. These landmarks become World Heritage Sites. They are protected from being destroyed by **urbanization,** pollution, tourism, and neglect.

▬ **Kayaking is a popular way to explore Lunenburg Harbour.**

You can learn more about UNESCO World Heritage Sites by visiting **http://whc.unesco.org**

▶Think about it ◀

World Heritage Sites belong to all people. They provide a link to the past. These sites also help people from many cultures connect with each other. Think about your own heritage. What landmarks are important to you? Think about the places that have shaped your life. Make a list of your personal heritage sites. The list might include your home, your grandparents' home, your school, or any other place that is special to you and your family. Next to each location on the list, write down why it is important to you.

Where in the World?

Lunenburg sits on a small peninsula on Nova Scotia's east coast. A peninsula is a piece of land that is almost surrounded by water. Lunenburg is about 90 kilometres southwest of Halifax, the province's capital city. Old Town Lunenburg is the oldest area of the town. It is where the town's first settlers built their homes. Some of Old Town Lunenburg's buildings were constructed more than 250 years ago.

Old Town Lunenburg is built on a steep hill overlooking Lunenburg Harbour. The harbour provides shelter and storage space for ships. Old Town Lunenburg's buildings reach from the waterfront to the top of the hill. From the ocean, it appears as if the rows of houses are stacked on top of one another. A smaller harbour, called Back Harbour, lies behind the town.

■ From the air, Old Town Lunenburg appears as a narrow strip of houses squeezed between the waters of Lunenburg Harbour and Back Harbour.

Puzzler

Nova Scotia is divided into 18 **counties**. Old Town Lunenburg is located in the county of Lunenburg. Both the town and the county are named for King George II of England. Along with being king, George was the Duke of Brunswick-Luneburg.

Visit **www.gov.ns.ca/playground**, and click on "People & Places." Use the map there to help you unscramble the county names below. Then, match the names to the numbers on the map.

ANSWERS: 1. Annapolis 2. Antigonish 3. Cape Breton 4. Colchester 5. Cumberland 6. Digby 7. Guysborough 8. Halifax 9. Hants 10. Inverness 11. Kings 12. Lunenburg 13. Picton 14. Queens 15. Richmond 16. Shelburne 17. Victoria 18. Yarmouth

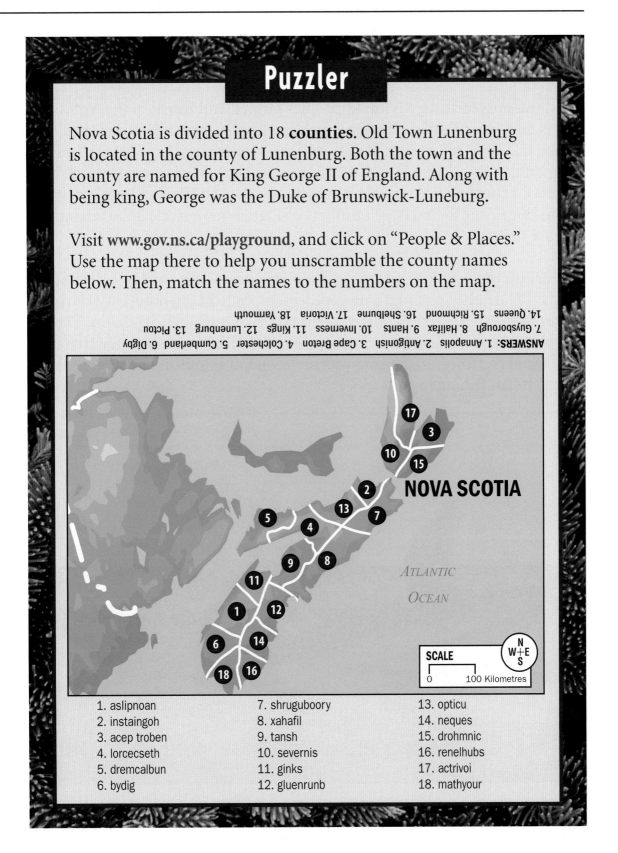

1. aslipnoan
2. instaingoh
3. acep troben
4. lorcecseth
5. dremcalbun
6. bydig
7. shruguboory
8. xahafil
9. tansh
10. severnis
11. ginks
12. gluenrunb
13. opticu
14. neques
15. drohmnic
16. renelhubs
17. actrivoi
18. mathyour

A Trip Back in Time

For thousands of years, **Mi'kmaq** peoples hunted and fished in the region that is now Nova Scotia. The first European to explore the land was John Cabot, in 1497. Cabot claimed the area for Great Britain. In 1604, explorers from France also claimed the land and nearby areas. France and Great Britain fought for control of Nova Scotia until 1723, when the British took control of the land. They forced large numbers of French settlers, called Acadians, to leave the area.

The British brought new settlers to populate Nova Scotia. In 1749, they built Halifax. Then, they planned a new settlement, called Lunenburg. It was to be a home for settlers recruited from Germany, France, and Switzerland. The first group of 1,453 settlers arrived on June 8, 1753. Most of the newcomers were farmers. However, the land was rocky and did not suit farming. Many people began fishing instead.

■ Fishers harvested many types of sea life in the waters off Lunenburg, including cod, crab, haddock, halibut, lobster, mackerel, prawns, and scallops.

Site Science

During the 1700s, British settlers built towns and villages in many parts of the world. They often used plans that were designed in advance. These plans were simple. Many were for communities that would be shaped in squares or rectangles. These communities were called model towns. Old Town Lunenburg is a model town. It is laid out in a rectangular grid pattern. Seven streets run straight north and south. These are crossed by nine streets running east and west. All the street corners in the town are perfectly square. They form equal-sized rectangular blocks. Like most model towns, planners left room for parks and other public spaces.

▬ Today, the original plan of Old Town Lunenburg is still intact.

FIND MORE ONLINE

See more of Lunenburg at www.lunenburgns.com.

Becoming a World Heritage Site

As Lunenburg grew, ships were needed for the fishing industry. They were also the main form of travel. Forests around Lunenburg provided wood for shipbuilding. The deep waters of Lunenburg Harbour were ideal for launching large vessels. By the early 1900s, Lunenburg was Canada's best-known shipbuilding centre. Many of the buildings still standing in Lunenburg were built during this period.

In the 1970s, people in Lunenburg wanted to protect the town's heritage. They recognized that its intact layout was rare. They knew that the town's fishing and shipbuilding history were important in Canada's development. In 1992, the Canadian Government made Old Town Lunenburg a National Historic Site. The government asked UNESCO to recognize the town. Old Town Lunenburg became a World Heritage Site in 1995.

▬ **A sign on the way into Lunenburg announces the town's UNESCO World Heritage status.**

Heritage Heroes

The Lunenburg Heritage Society was formed in 1972 to preserve and promote heritage in Old Town Lunenburg. It has helped build the town's first public library and an art gallery. To protect the look of the town, the society has helped make laws to ensure that all new construction matches existing styles.

The Heritage Society has published many books and pamphlets about the history of Lunenburg and Nova Scotia. In 2000, the group opened the Knaut-Rhuland House Museum in one of Lunenburg's historic homes. Here, visitors learn what life was like in early Lunenburg. They can view furniture, clothing, and other household objects from that time.

Today, the Lunenburg Heritage Society has about 150 members. They raise money for preservation projects in Lunenburg. The group plans heritage activities, such as festivals and tours.

At the Knaut-Rhuland House Museum, members of the Heritage Society dress in historic clothing to teach visitors about Lunenburg's past. The society has rebuilt many of the town's original buildings, including the bandstand that was first made in 1889.

World Heritage in

CANADA

There are more than 800 UNESCO World Heritage Sites in 138 countries around the globe. Canada has 14 of these sites. Seven are natural sites, and seven are cultural sites. Each is believed to be of outstanding heritage value to all people around the world. Look at the map. Are any of these sites near your home? Have you visited any of them? Learn more about World Heritage Sites in Canada by visiting www.pc.gc.ca/progs/spm-whs/itm2-/index_e.asp.

Head-Smashed-In Buffalo Jump (Alberta)
- A large, ancient cliff once used by the Plains Aboriginal Peoples to hunt bison on the Prairies
- One of the oldest and best-preserved buffalo jumps in North America

Historic District of Old-Quebec (Quebec)
- The only walled city north of Mexico
- The birthplace of French culture in North America

Kluane/Wrangell-St Elias/Glacier Bay/ Tatshenshini-Alsek (British Columbia, Yukon, and Alaska)
- A massive icefield on the border between British Columbia, the Yukon, and Alaska

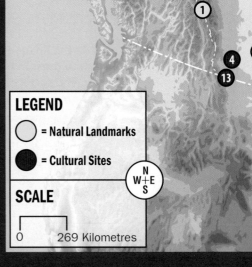

UNITED STATES OF AMERICA

YUKON

⑥

⑨

BRITISH COLUMBIA

⑫

ALBERTA

①

②

④

⑬

LEGEND

◯ = Natural Landmarks

● = Cultural Sites

N W+E S

SCALE

0   269 Kilometres

① Canadian Rocky Mountain Parks (Alberta and British Columbia)

② Dinosaur Provincial Park (Alberta)

③ Gros Morne National Park (Newfoundland and Labrador)

④ Head-Smashed-In Buffalo Jump (Alberta)

CANADA

NORTHWEST
TERRITORIES

NUNAVUT

(14)

SASKATCHEWAN

NEWFOUNDLAND
AND LABRADOR

(7)

MANITOBA

(3)

PRINCE
EDWARD
ISLAND

ONTARIO

QUEBEC

(8)

NEW
BRUNSWICK

NOVA
SCOTIA

(5)

(10)

UNITED STATES
OF AMERICA

(11)

5 The Historic District of
Old-Quebec (Quebec)

6 Kluane/Wrangell-St Elias/Glacier
Bay/Tatshenshini-Alsek (British
Columbia, Yukon, and Alaska)

7 L'Anse aux Meadows National
Historic Site (Newfoundland
and Labrador)

8 Miguasha National Park (Quebec)

9 Nahanni National Park Reserve
(Northwest Territories)

10 Old Town Lunenburg (Nova Scotia)

11 Rideau Canal (Ontario)

12 SGang Gwaay (British Columbia)

13 Waterton Glacier International
Peace Park (Alberta and Montana)

14 Wood Buffalo National Park
(Alberta and Northwest Territories)

Natural Wonders

Many of Lunenburg's natural features were formed by glaciers moving over the land about 20,000 years ago. The glaciers carved rocky beaches into Nova Scotia's coastline. They deposited rocks and other sediments in the form of **drumlins**. These unique landforms create the many green hills found around Lunenburg today.

When settlers first came to the area, the drumlins near Lunenburg were covered in forests of American beech, sugar maple, and red oak trees. Over time, settlers cleared the forests to build the town and supply the shipbuilding industry. They used the cleared drumlins for farming. Some of this land is still farmed. Other areas are used for growing balsam fir trees. These are used for Christmas trees. There are so many firs in Lunenburg County that it is often called the "Christmas Tree Capital of the World."

▬ From a distance, the drumlins around Lunenburg give the land a wavy appearance.

FIND MORE ONLINE

Learn more about how glaciers work at http://nsidc.org/glaciers.

Creature Feature

The Atlantic cod is found in the cool waters of the North Atlantic Ocean. It is one of the most important animals in Canadian history. In the late 1400s, explorers from Europe discovered Atlantic cod in waters off Canada's Atlantic coast. Many fishers from Europe travelled to the area to fish for Atlantic cod. Over time, they built settlements along the coast. These fishing communities, including the town of Lunenburg, marked the beginning of British settlement in what is now Canada.

The Atlantic cod is one of 59 **species** of codfish. It has small, smooth scales on its back. The scales can be grey, green, brown, or red. Atlantic cod have three fins on their back and two fins on their tail. They have a slim, whisker-like barbel on their chin, which they use to find food in the water.

▬ There were once so many Atlantic cod that they were scooped from the water in buckets. Today, some scientists believe that Atlantic cod are at risk of dying out due to over-fishing.

Cultural Treasures

In 1753, **Protestants** from Germany, France, and Switzerland settled in Lunenburg. In the 1780s, British settlers moving north from the United States joined them. Today, Lunenburg culture is a blend of traditions passed down by these groups. *Fraktur*, the German art of book-decoration, is practised alongside traditional British music styles. Carpentry around town reflects a mix of German, French, Swiss, and British styles.

Throughout the year, the town's seafaring culture is celebrated with special events. The Fishermen's Picnic and Reunion began in 1918. It is held each summer. Fishing demonstrations, live music, sports, and traditional foods are part of this event. The Lunenburg Folk Harbour Festival is held in August. Local musicians play traditional fiddle music and sing Lunenburg sea shanties. Shanties are songs about a person's relationship with the sea.

■ Water sports, including boat races and the lobster crate race, are an important part of the Fishermen's Picnic and Reunion.

Telling Tales

Lunenburg is known for its stories. Many, such as "The Treasure of Oak Island," have seafaring themes.

Three boys from Lunenburg rowed out to Oak Island 200 years ago. They left their boat on the shore and walked toward some trees. They saw an oak tree with a large ship's pulley hanging from a branch. The brush around the tree had been cut down. The boys thought this meant something was buried under the tree.

The boys set to work digging. Late in the day, they found oak beams in the pit. The boys returned home and told their families what they had found. The next day, some men joined the boys on their return to Oak Island. The group made the pit much wider and deeper. Soon, they reached a barrier of ship's putty. They believed treasure was on the other side. As they broke through the putty, water flooded the pit. Those digging barely escaped.

To this day, many treasure hunters have returned to Oak Island to dig for treasure. None have found what lies at the bottom of the pit.

Amazing Attractions

Old Town Lunenburg is a colourful place. Many of the homes are painted in bright shades of red, green, and blue, trimmed with white. Most were built for sea captains or **merchants** in the 1700s and 1800s. Eight date back to the original settlement of 1753. A unique style of window, called the Lunenburg bump, is seen on many of these buildings. The Lunenburg bump is placed over a door. It has many window panels that are angled to let in more light.

The waterfront area was once the heart of Lunenburg's shipbuilding industry. It remains the town's centre of activity. The **dory** workshop is still used to build and repair ships. Nearby, the fisherman's memorial lists the names of all Lunenburg fishers who have lost their lives to the sea since 1890. *Bluenose II* is often seen anchored in Lunenburg Harbour. It is an exact copy of the *Bluenose*, a well-known ship that was built in Lunenburg. The *Bluenose* appears on the Canadian dime.

■ The Dory Shop has used the same techniques to build dory boats since 1917.

Featured Attraction

The Fisheries Museum of the Atlantic is housed in an old factory along the waterfront. It is filled with sea chests, **navigational** tools, and ocean charts. The museum has the largest collection of *Bluenose* items in the world. Educational displays and movies teach visitors about the history of fishing in the Atlantic. An aquarium allows visitors to see and touch starfish and other sea life. Outside, visitors can help launch a model boat into the harbour or tour a ship that was once used for fishing.

Issues in Heritage

Preserving Old Town Lunenburg is a challenge. The number of people who live in the town year-round is decreasing. There are fewer people to look after historic buildings during the cold months, when they may be damaged by rain, snow, wind, and ice. Many buildings require repairs. People who live in town only part of the year do not want to spend large sums of money on these projects. Town leaders are working hard to make sure people in Lunenburg take an interest in preserving the town's heritage and **restoring** their homes.

More and more people are coming to Lunenburg for the spring and summer months. Large numbers of visitors can damage the buildings and the environment. There are fewer places for visitors to stay each summer. Some people want to build **condominium** apartments along the waterfront to house tourists. Others are concerned that this will ruin the historic nature of Old Town Lunenburg.

▬ Upkeep on the historic buildings in Lunenburg can be quite costly.

FIND MORE ONLINE

Learn about ongoing projects to protect Old Town Lunenburg at: www.lunenburgheritagesociety.ca.

Should condominiums be built on the waterfront in Old Town Lunenburg?

YES	NO
New people living in the town will help support local stores and services. This will help the town keep its unique, historic character.	Large numbers of people living in condominiums will put pressure on services and cause historic buildings to wear down faster.
Shipbuilding has been replaced by tourism as the most important industry in Old Town Lunenburg.	The condominiums will be empty during the fall and winter months, when tourism is slow.
The outside of the condominium buildings will have the same architectural features and paint as the heritage buildings.	Condominiums are much larger than the other buildings in Old Town. They will ruin the historic look of the town.

Think about this issue. Are there any possible solutions that would satisfy both sides of the debate?

Plan a Model Town

Imagine you are living 250 years in the past. King George II has asked you to plan a new settlement on the land where your town now sits. The settlement will be based on the same model town plan used at Lunenburg.

Materials Needed

Large piece of paper (28 centimetres by 43 cm or larger), a pencil, a ruler, coloured pencils or felt markers, stencils in the shape of a circle, a triangle, and a rectangle

1 Think about the land where the settlement will be built. What natural features are nearby? Are there hills, rivers, or a forest? Draw these features on your paper. Decide where the town will be in relation to these features.

2 Draw the borders of the settlement. Decide if the town should be enclosed by walls for protection. Draw the walls around the outside of your town.

3 Use the ruler to draw the streets of the town. Draw seven streets running north and south. Draw nine streets running across them east and west.

4 Add special constructions. For example, if the settlement is a harbour town like Lunenburg, draw docks for the ships.

5 Now, think about the people who will live in the town. Use square or rectangle stencils to draw buildings. Draw small squares for homes. Draw larger squares for other buildings, such as a store, a school, a hospital, or a shipbuilder. Leave space for public areas, such as parks and a town square.

6 Give the town a name. It is now ready for settlers.

Quiz

1. Where did the first Lunenburg settlers come from?
2. True or false? The coastline of Nova Scotia was formed in the eighteenth century.
3. What animal led to settlement of Canada's Atlantic coast?
4. What group of people did the British remove from Nova Scotia in the mid-1700s?
5. What is the name of a well-known building feature in Lunenburg?

ANSWERS: 1. Germany, France, and Switzerland 2. False. The coastline was created 20,000 years ago during the ice age. 3. the Atlantic cod 4. the Acadians 5. the Lunenburg bump

Further Research

You can find more information on Old Town Lunenburg at your local library or on the Internet.

Libraries

Most libraries have computers that connect to a database for researching information. If you input a key word, you will be provided with a list of books in the library that contain information on that topic. Non-fiction books are arranged numerically, using their call number. Fiction books are organized alphabetically by the author's last name.

Websites

See the sail plan of the *Bluenose II* at www.schoonerbluenose2.ca/sail-plan.html.

Join the UNESCO World Heritage in Young Hands Project for students at http://whc.unesco.org/education.

Glossary

colonial: related to life in a colony, or a community formed by people who have left their own country to settle in another

condominium: a housing structure with many units that are owned separately

counties: areas of a province that are divided for the purpose of government

culture: the characteristics, beliefs, and practices of a racial, religious, or social group

dory: a wooden boat with oars

drumlins: long, oval hills made of material left by large bodies of ice moving over the land

merchants: people who make a living by buying and selling goods for profit

Mi'kmaq: an Aboriginal group living in the Maritime provinces and parts of Quebec

navigational: related to the science of determining the position and course of boats, ships, and aircraft

preserved: protected from injury, loss, or ruin

Protestants: members of any Christian church other than the Roman Catholic Church or the Orthodox Church

restoring: bringing something back to its original state

species: a group of plants or animals that share the same characteristics

urbanization: the movement of people out of the countryside and into cities

Index

Acadians 8, 23
Atlantic cod 15, 23
Atlantic Ocean 7, 15, 19

Bluenose I 18, 19
Bluenose II 18, 23

culture 4, 5, 12, 16

Fisheries Museum of the Atlantic 19
fishing 4, 8, 10, 15, 16, 19

history 4, 10, 11, 15, 19

issues 20, 21

King George II 7, 22

Lunenburg bump 18, 23
Lunenburg Heritage Society 11

Mi'kmaq 8
model town 4, 9, 22
music 16

Nova Scotia 4, 6, 7, 8, 11, 13, 14, 23

shipbuilding 4, 10, 14, 18, 21
stories 17

United Nations Educational, Scientific, and Cultural Organization (UNESCO) 5, 10, 12, 23

waterfront 6, 18, 19, 20, 21
World Heritage Sites 4, 5, 10, 12, 13, 23